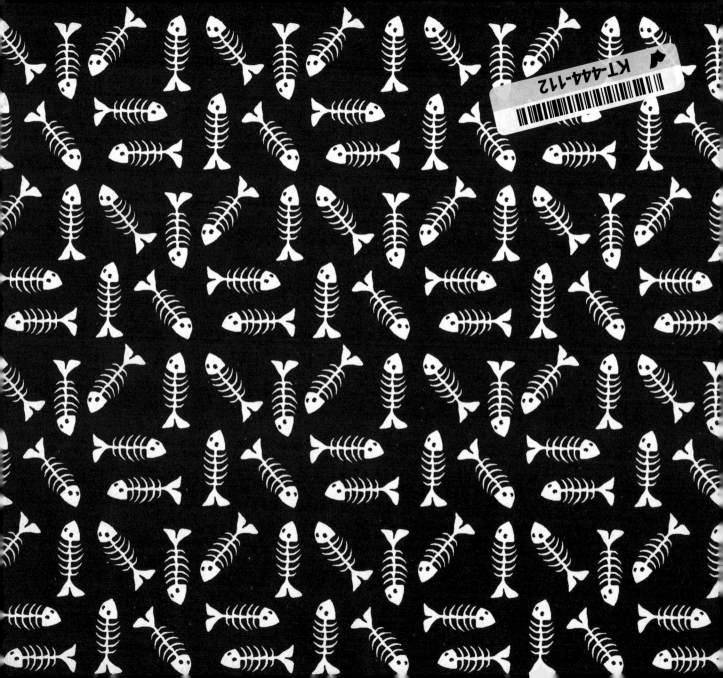

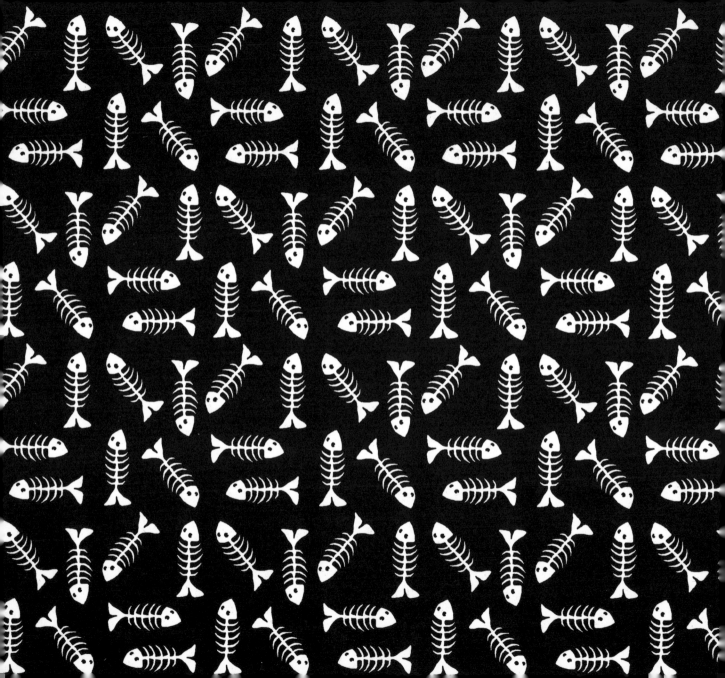

Felines

Felines

great
poets
on
notorious
cats

WITH LINOCUTS BY MARTHA PAULOS

CHRONICLE BOOKS ▪ SAN FRANCISCO

Grateful acknowledgment is made for permission to reprint the following copyrighted works:

The Cat from MANY LONG YEARS AGO by Ogden Nash. Copyright 1933 by Ogden Nash. By permission of Little, Brown and Company.

My Cat, Mrs. Lick-a-chin from YOU READ TO ME, I'LL READ TO YOU by John Ciardi. Copyright © 1962 by Myra J. Ciardi. Reprinted by permission of Harper Collins Publishers.

Cat on the Mat from THE ADVENTURES OF TOM BOMBADIL by J.R.R. Tolkien. Copyright © 1962 by George Allen & Unwin, Ltd. Reprinted by permission of Houghton Mifflin Company. All rights reserved.

As You Were Saying by Alice Adams. Copyright © 1992 by Alice Adams. Reprinted by permission of the author.

Nine Fat Cats in Little Italy by Herbert Mitgang. Copyright © 1992 by Herbert Mitgang. Reprinted by permission of the author.

The Cat and the Moon from THE COLLECTED POEMS OF W.B. YEATS: A NEW EDITION, edited by Richard J. Finneran. Copyright 1919 by Macmillan Publishing Company, renewed 1947 by Bertha Georgie Yeats. Reprinted with permission of Macmillan Publishing Company.

Peter from COLLECTED POEMS by Marianne Moore. Copyright 1935 by Marianne Moore, renewed 1963 by Marianne Moore and T.S. Eliot. Reprinted with permission of Macmillan Publishing Company.

This Is My Chair from THE HONORABLE CAT by Paul Gallico. Copyright © 1972 by Paul Gallico and Mathemata Anstalt. Reprinted by permission of Crown Publishers, Inc.

Cat by Jean Cocteau. Copyright © 1953 by WAKE. Printed by permission of Seymour Lawrence, sole owner of Wake Editions.

Cat Morgan Introduces Himself from OLD POSSUM'S BOOK OF PRACTICAL CATS, copyright 1939 by T.S. Eliot and renewed 1967 by Esme Valerie Eliot. Reprinted by permission of Harcourt Brace Jovanovich, Inc.

Cat's Dream translated by Alastair Reid in A NEW DECADE: POEMS 1958–1967 by Pablo Neruda. English translation copyright © 1969 by Alastair Reid. Used by permission of Grove Press, Inc.

Poem by William Carlos Williams from THE COLLECTED POEMS OF WILLIAM CARLOS WILLIAMS, 1909–1939, VOL. I. Copyright 1938 by New Directions Publishing Corporation.

Printed in Japan.
ISBN: 0-8118-0103-9
Library of Congress Cataloging in Publication Data available.
Book and cover design: Fly Productions
Distributed in Canada by Raincoast Books, 112 East Third Avenue, Vancouver, B.C. V5T 1C8

10   9   8   7   6   5   4   3   2   1

Chronicle Books
275 Fifth Street
San Francisco, CA 94103

F🐱Y
PRODUCTIONS

CONTENTS

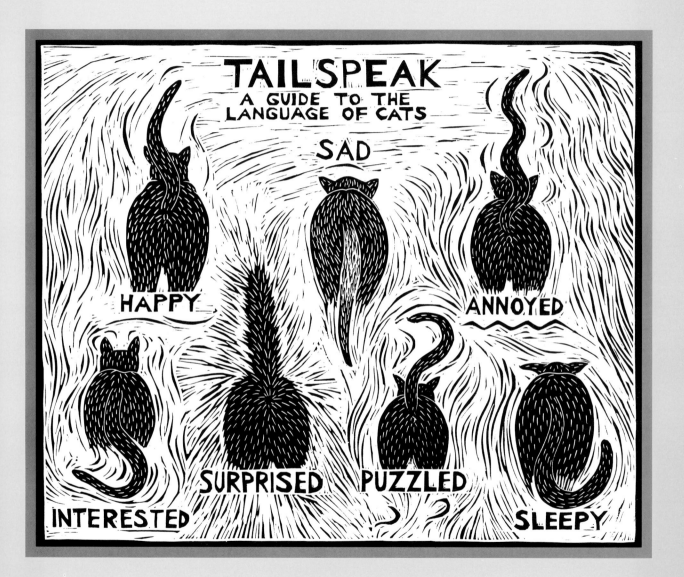

The Cat

You get a wife, you get a house,

Eventually you get a mouse.

You get some words regarding mice,

You get a kitty in a trice.

By two A.M. or thereabout,

The mouse is in, the cat is out.

It dawns upon you, in your cot,

The mouse is silent, the cat is not.

Instead of Pussy, says your spouse,

You should have bought another mouse.

Kitten and Fallen Leaves

See the kitten on the wall,
Sporting with the leaves that fall,
Withered leaves — one — two — and three —
From the lofty elder tree!
Through the calm and frosty air
Of this morning bright and fair,
Eddying round and round they sink
Softly, slowly: one might think
From the motions that are made,
Every little leaf conveyed
Sylph or fairy hither tending,
To this lower world descending,
Each invisible and mute,

In his wavering parachute.
— But the kitten, how she starts,
Crouches, stretches, paws and darts
First at one, and then its fellow,
Just as light and just as yellow!
Where are many now — now one —
Now they stop and there are none:
What intenseness of desire
In her upward eye of fire!
With a tiger-leap half-way
Now she meets the coming prey,
Lets it go as fast, and then
Has it in her power again:
Now she works with three or four,
Like an Indian conjuror;
Quick as he in feats of art,
Far beyond in joy of heart.
When her antics played in the eye

Of a thousand standers-by,
Clapping hands with shout and stare,
What would little Tabby care
For the plaudits of the crowd?
Over-happy to be proud,
Over-wealthy in the treasure
Of her own exceeding pleasure.

The Tom Cat

At midnight in the alley
    A tomcat comes to wail,
And he chants the hate of a million years
    As he swings his snaky tail.

Malevolent, bony, brindled,
    Tiger and devil and bard,
His eyes are coals from middle of hell,
    And his heart is black and hard.

He twists and crouches and capers
    And bares his curved sharp claws,
And he sings to the stars of the jungle nights
    Ere cities were, or laws.

Beast from a world primeval,
    He and his leaping clan,
When the blotched red moon leers over the roofs
    give voice to their scorn of man.

He will lie on a rug tomorrow
    And lick his silky fur,
And veil the brute in his yellow eyes
    And play he's tame, and purr.

But at midnight in the alley
    He will crouch again and wail,
And beat the time for demon's song
    With the swing of his demon's tail.

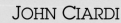

My Cat, Mrs. Lick-a-chin

Some of the cats I know about
Spend a little time in and a lot of time out.
Or a lot of time out and a little time in.
By *my* cat, Mrs. Lick-a-chin,
Never knows *where* she wants to be.
If I let her in she looks at me
And begins to sing that she wants to go out.
So I open the door and she looks about
And begins to sing, "Please let me in!"

Poor silly Mrs. Lick-a-chin!

The thing about cats as you might find,
Is that no one knows what they have in mind.

And I'll tell you something about that:
No one knows it less than my cat.

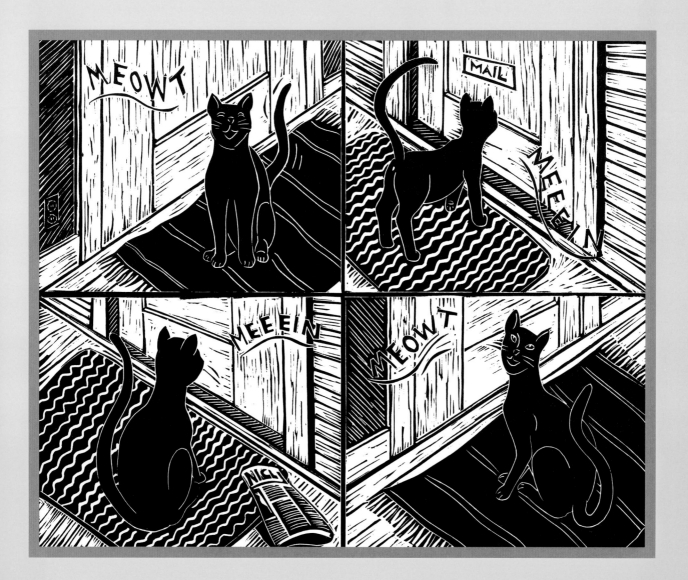

Cat on the Mat

The fat cat on the mat
   may seem to dream
of nice mice that suffice
   for him, or cream;
but he is free, maybe,
   walks in thought
unbowed, proud, where loud
   roared and fought
his kin, lean and slim,
   or deep in den
in the East feasted on beasts
   and tender men.

The giant lion with iron
  claw in paw,
and huge ruthless tooth
  in gory jaw;
the pard dark-starred
  fleet upon feet,
that oft soft from aloft
  leaps on his meet
where words loom in gloom —
  far now they be
  fierce and free,
  and tamed is he;
but fat cat on the mat
kept as pet
he does not forget.

As You Were Saying

Telling me about Rosebud
(But not saying, 'put to sleep')
"A beautiful cat, so beautiful,
Even as she died,"
You say, on the phone,
And that was true, I had met her:
A lithe lovely shy tabby cat,
Hiding under the bedclothes, darting out.

But at that moment
As I listen, from California,
In the Truckee River I see two fat brown ducks,
Serene and elegant, and vastly silly.
How I wish you were here to come and look!
As they veer away from rocks
And sail downstream,
Like gamblers, headed for Reno.

                                        for Richard Poirier

Nine Fat Cats in Little Italy

Say buon giorn to fatso Toni
    She likes to gorge on peperoni.
Ignazio gatto feels so lucky
    When he's stuffed with molti gnocchi.
Our favorite kitty Carolina
    Mangia bene on pastina.
Caruso cat sings for salami
    With parmesan and vermicelli.
The bandit tomcat Lee Gumba'ro
    Steals the sausage of San Gennaro.
Padrone cat Marloni Brando
    Prays last rites for cannellono.
The royal feline Medici
    Drinks champagne with biscotti.
When it comes to frutt' di mari
    A cat called Est chews calamari.
Laura loves her antipasta
    Prosciutto, pesce and polenta,
    Risotto, ragu, rigatoni
    And Yankee Doodle macaroni!

A CAT'S ENTERTAINMENT

Untitled

She sights a bird, she chuckles,
She flattens, then she crawls,
She runs without the look of feet,
Her eyes increase to balls,

Her jaws stir, twitching, hungry,
Her teeth can hardly stand.
She leaps — but robin leaps the first!
Ah, pussy of the sand,

The hopes so juicy ripening,
You almost bathed your tongue
When bliss dissolved a hundred wings
And fled with every one!

The Cat and the Moon

The cat went here and there
And the moon spun round like a top,
And the nearest kin of the moon,
The creeping cat, looked up.
Black Minnaloushe stared at the moon,
For, wander and wail as he would,
The pure cold light in the sky
Troubled his animal blood.
Minnaloushe runs in the grass
Lifting his delicate feet.
Do you dance, Minnaloushe, do you dance?
When two close kindred meet,

What better than call a dance?
Maybe the moon may learn,
Tired of that courtly fashion,
A new dance turn.
Minnaloushe creeps through the grass
From moonlit place to place,
The sacred moon overhead
Has taken a new phase.
Does Minnaloushe know that his pupils
Will pass from change to change,
And that from round to crescent,
From crescent to round they range?
Minnaloushe creeps through the grass
Alone, important and wise,
And lifts to the changing moon
His changing eyes.

In Honor of Taffy Topaz

Taffy, the topaz-colored cat,
Thinks now of this and now of that,
But chiefly of his meals.
Asparagus, and cream, and fish,
Are objects of his Freudian wish;
What you don't give, he steals.

His gallant heart is strongly stirred
By the clink of plate or flight of bird,
He has a plumy tail;
At night he treads on stealthy pad
As merry as Sir Galahad
A-seeking of the Grail.

His amiable amber eyes
Are very friendly, very wise;
Like Buddha, grave and fat,
He sits, regardless of applause,
And thinking, as he kneads his paws,
What fun to be a cat!

My Cat

My pretty cat to my heart I hold,
My heart ever warm to her;
Let me look thine eyes of agate and gold;
Thy claws keep sheathed in fur.

My finger strokes thy head, and thrills
Thy back that arches higher;
My touch with quivering rapture fills
Thy veins electric fire.

I dream of my love; her eyes like thine,
Profound and cold, sweet cat of mine,
My Soul dart-wounds fret.

A subtle air, a deadly sweet
Breathes round her, and from head to feet
Envelopes my brunette.

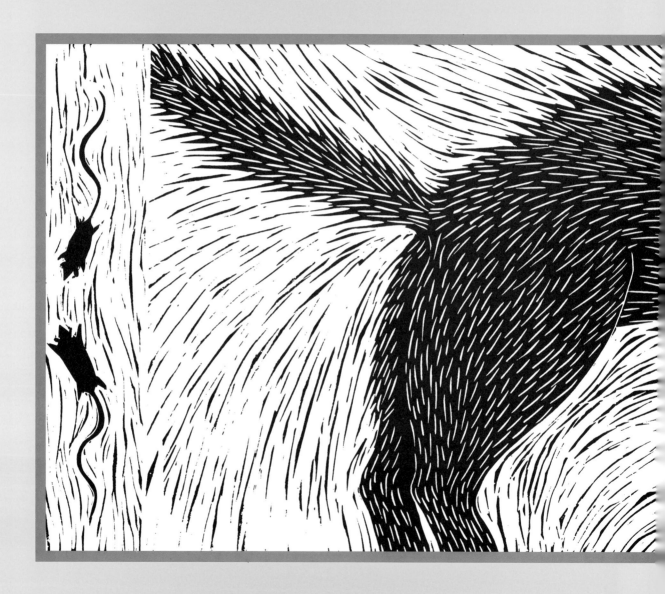

MARIANNE MOORE

Peter

Strong and slippery,
built for the midnight grass-party
confronted by four cats he sleeps his time away —
the detached first claw on the foreleg corresponding
to the thumb, retracted to its tip; the small tuft of fronds
or katydid-legs above each eye numbering all units
in each group; the shadbones regularly set about the mouth
to droop or rise in unison like porcupine-quills.
He lets himself be flattened out by gravity,
as seaweed is tamed and weakened by the sun,
compelled when extended, to lie stationary.
Sleep is the result of his delusion that one must

do as well as one can for oneself,

sleep — epitome of what is to him the end of life.

Demonstrate on him how the lady placed a forked stick

on the innocuous neck-sides of the dangerous southern snake.

One need not try to stir him up; his prune-shaped head

and alligator-eyes are not party to the joke.

Lifted and handled, he may be dangled like an eel

or set up on the forearm like a mouse;

his eyes bisected by pupils of a pin's width,

are flickeringly exhibited, then covered up.

May be? I should have said might have been;

when he has been got the better of in a dream —

as in a fight with nature of with cats, we all know it.

Profound sleep is not with him a fixed illusion.

Springing about with frog-like accuracy, with jerky cries

when taken in hand, he is himself again;

to sit caged by the rungs of a domestic chair

would be unprofitable — human. What is the good of hypocrisy?
It is permissible to choose one's employment,
to abandon the nail, or roly-poly,
 when it shows signs of being no longer a pleasure,
 to score the nearby magazine with a double line of strokes.
He can talk but insolently says nothing. What of it?
When one is frank, one's very presence is a compliment.
It is clear that he can see the virtue of naturalness,
that he does not regard the published fact as a surrender.
As for the disposition invariably to affront,
an animal with claws should have an opportunity to use them.
The eel-like extension of the trunk into tail is not an accident.
To leap, to lengthen out, divide the air, to purloin, to pursue.
To tell the hen: fly over the fence, go in the wrong way
in your perturbation — this is life;
to do less would be nothing but dishonesty.

Oscar Wilde

The Sphinx

In a dim corner of my room for longer than my fancy thinks,
A beautiful and silent Sphinx has watched me through the shifting gloom.

Inviolate and immobile she does not rise, she does not stir
For silver moons are naught to her and naught to her the suns that reel.

Red follows grey across the air, the waves of moonlight ebb and flow,
But with the Dawn she does not go and in the night-time she is there.

Dawn follows Dawn and Nights grow old and all the while this curious cat
Lies crouching on the Chinese mat with eyes of satin rimmed with gold.

Upon the mat she lies and leers and on the tawny throat of her
Flutters the soft and silky fur ripples to her pointed ears.

Come forth, my lovely seneschal! so somnolent, so statuesque!
Come forth you exquisite grotesque! half woman and half animal!

Come forth my lovely languorous Sphinx! and put your head upon my knee!
    And let me stroke your throat and see your body spotted like the Lynx!

And let me touch those curving claws of yellow ivory, and grasp
The tail that like a monstrous Asp coils round your heavy velvet paws!

This Is My Chair

This is my chair.
Go away and sit somewhere else.
This one is all my own.
It is the only thing in your house that I possess
And insist upon possessing.
Everything else therein is yours.
My dish,
My toys,
My basket,
My scratching post and my Ping-Pong ball;
You provided them for me.
This chair I selected for myself.
I like it,
It suits me.
You have the sofa,
The stuffed chair
And the footstool.
I don't go and sit on them do I?
Then why cannot you leave me mine,
And let us have no further argument?

Cat

By the fire, like drifting reddish goldfish,

the cat dozed, within itself.

If, by mischance, I were to stir,

the cat might change to something else.

The spinning-wheel of ancient magic

must never be allowed to stick:

and changing itself into a princess

is, for the cat, a minor trick.

T. S. Eliot

Cat Morgan Introduces Himself

I once was a Pirate what sailed the 'igh seas —
　　But now I've retired as a com-mission-aire:
And that's how you find me a-takin' my ease
　　And keepin' the door in a Bloomsbury Square.

I'm partial to partridges, likewise to grouse,
　　And I favour that Devonshire cream in a bowl;
But I'm allus content with a drink on the 'ouse
　　And a bit o'cold fish when I done me patrol.

I ain't got much polish, me manners is gruff,
　　but I've got a good coat, and keep myself smart;
And everyone says, and I guess that's enough:
　　'You can't but like Morgan, 'e's got a kind 'art.'

I got knocked about on the Barbary Coast,
    And me voice it ain't no sich melliferous horgan;
But yet I can state, and I'm not one to boast,
    That some of the gals is dead keen on old Morgan.

So if you 'ave business with Faber — or Faber —
    I'll give you this tip, and it's worth a lot more:
You'll save yourself time, and you'll spare yourself labour
    If jist you make friends with the Cat at the door.

                                MORGAN.

Cat's Dream

How neatly a cat sleeps,
sleeps with its paws and its substance,
sleeps with its wicked claws,
and with its ruthless blood,
sleeps with all the rings —
a series of burnt circles —
which form the odd geology
of its sand-colored tail.

I should sleep like a cat,
with all the fur of time,
with a tongue rough as flint,

— 53 —

with the dry sex of fire;
and after speaking to no one,
stretch myself over the world,
over the roofs and landscapes,
with a passionate desire
to hunt the rats in my dreams.

I have seen how the cat asleep
would undulate, how the night
flowed through it like dark water;
and at times, it was going to fall
or possibly plunge into
the bare deserted snowdrifts.
Sometimes it grew so much in sleep
like a tiger's great-grandfather,
and would leap in the darkness over
rooftops, clouds and volcanoes.

Sleep, sleep, cat of the night,

with episcopal ceremony

and your stone-hewn mustache.

Take care of all our dreams;

control the obscurity

of our slumbering prowess

with your relentless heart

and the great ruff of your tail.

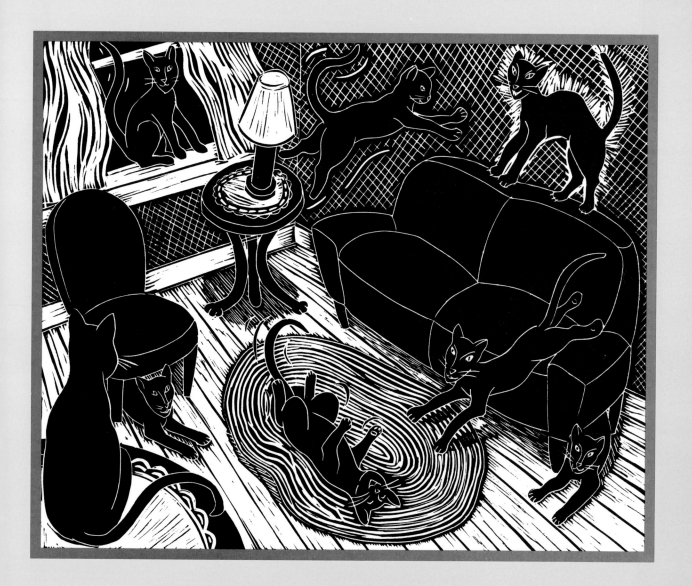

Poem

As the cat
climbed over
the top of

the jamcloset
first the right
forefoot

carefully
then the hind
stepped down

into the pit of
the empty
flower pot

Woman and Cat

They were at play, she and her cat,
And it was marvelous to mark
The white paw and the white hand pat
Each other in the deepening dark.

The stealthy little lady hid
Under the mitten's silken sheath
Her dainty agate nails that shred,
The silk-like dagger-points of death.

The cat purred primly and drew in
Her claws that were of steel filed thin:
The devil was in it all the same.

And in the boudoir, while a shout
Of laughter in the air rang out,
Four sparks of phosphor shone like flame.

SINCLAIR LEWIS

The Cat's Prayer

This is a cat that sleeps at night,
That takes delight
In visions bright,
And not a vagrant that creeps at night
On box-cars by the river.
This is a sleepy cat to purr
And rarely stir
Its shining fur;
This is a cat whose softest purr
Means salmon, steaks and liver.

That is a cat respectable,
Connectable
With selectable
Felines respectable,
Whose names would make you quiver.
That is a cat of piety,

Not satiety,
But sobriety.
Its very purr is of piety
And thanks to its Feline Giver.

And this is how it prays:

`Ancient of days
With whiskers torrendous
Hark to our praise,
Lick and defend us.
Lo, how we bring to Thee,
Sweet breasts of mouses;
Hark how we sing to Thee,
Filling all houses
With ardent miaouses,
Until it arouses
All mankind to battery.
Thou of the golden paws,
Thou of the silver claws,
Thy tail is the comets' cause,
King of all cattery!'

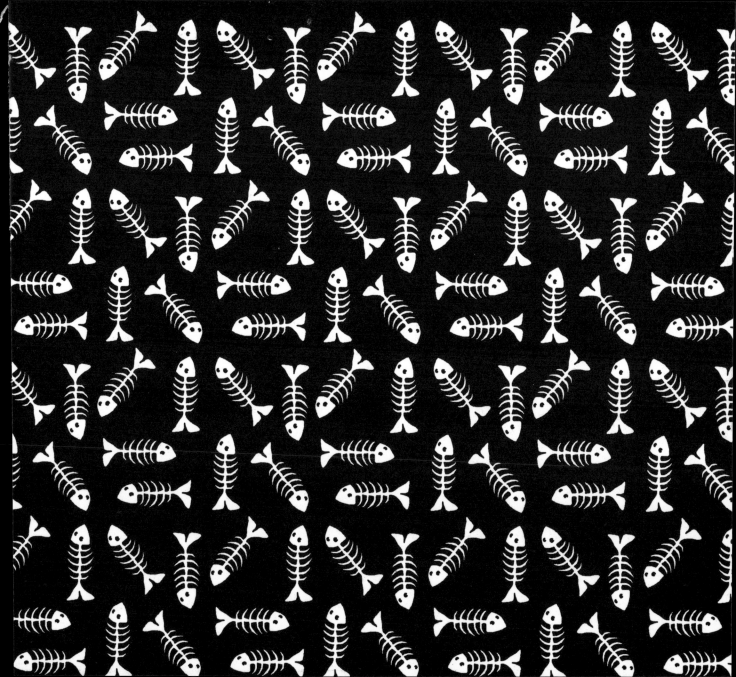